All th
Ahead

All the Days Ahead

A Testament of Bereavement

—◎—

FREDA BAKER

DARTON, LONGMAN AND TODD
London

First published in 1992 by
Darton, Longman and Todd Ltd
89 Lillie Road, London SW6 1UD

ISBN 0–232–51968–4

A catalogue record for this book is available
from the British Library

Designed by Sandie Boccacci

Phototypeset in 10/12pt Palatino by Intype, London
Printed and bound in Great Britain
at the University Press, Cambridge

FOR ERIC

Never too late

But (when so sad thou canst not sadder)
Cry; – and upon thy so sore loss
Shall shine the traffic of Jacob's ladder
Pitched betwixt Heaven and Charing Cross.

Yea, in the night, my Soul, my daughter,
Cry, – clinging Heaven by the hems;
And lo, Christ walking on the water
Not of Gennesareth, but Thames!

Francis Thompson

Preface

It is not easy, and usually not very wise, to share one's most secret thoughts and feelings with others. My reason for doing so in this book is my awareness of being, not an island, but part of that great continent of the bereaved. We have all experienced personally and with deep sorrow the shattering trauma of the death of someone near to us. Each in our own way finally manages to come through and to begin to live again, and it occurred to me that in sharing my own experiences perhaps someone – somewhere – might be helped along the way.

Freda Baker

February

5th

Death was no stranger to me when you died.

People came. I told them that I was 'all right' because the shock was too immense to express. I and the house and the world were an abyss. The emptiness was unbelievable.

Yet I coped. I was 'all right', and I coped. I filled in all the DSS forms, made all the arrangements, spoke calmly and coherently.

I coped because there is a power within stronger than me. Stronger, yet part of me. There is the big 'I' capable of overcoming any and every situation and circumstance, and the little 'me' who would crumple like a tired child. So often it takes sorrow or crisis to discover this power within ourselves.

Now I am living in an awareness of days – all the days ahead. Previously I was living in no-man's-land, where there is no day or night, no yesterday, today or tomorrow.

This, then, is Day One of a new era . . .

⟿ *6th* ⟿

The policewoman was young. She said what she had to say as soon as she saw me.

'I don't believe it,' I said. 'I don't believe it . . . I DON'T BELIEVE IT . . .'

'No,' she said. 'You won't believe it yet.'

But it had to be told. I had to tell them. All of them. That you had collapsed in the town . . . that you were found to be dead on arrival at the hospital.

She suggested tea. I didn't even take it in. I didn't make any. Neither did she. I 'phoned and 'phoned. And 'phoned.

She lit a cigarette, and waited. 'I don't like to leave you,' she said.

How you would have joked with her . . .

The clergyman who called said I must eat. But he wasn't really a clergyman. He was a lay reader. The Vicar was busy in his many parishes.

They wondered if I would mind if the lay reader took the burial service. Mind? I thought immediately of you; how pleased you would have been to have this ordinary elderly man conduct the necessary proceedings (which you would have thought unnecessary anyway). You who were always so wary of the clergy.

This was one of many small comforts. A pity, though, he had to dress up in robes, billowing about him in the wind as he stood there in the gateway of the church, waiting for us. You would have preferred him without them.

The two sedate cats sitting opposite, waiting and watching, would have pleased you.

After the funeral we drank tea and ate cake and everyone laughed and talked as if you had not died. You mustn't be hurt. You would be, I think. Please don't mind it. Underneath everyone cares. They just have to carry on living.

Later I laughed too. A lot. I'm sorry. I could hear myself, but I couldn't stop. They said I either had to laugh or to cry, and I had no tears. Once I wept because my feelings were hurt, but for you I could not weep . . .

We have to carry on living. I'm trying to. I even remember to take my blood-pressure pill each day.

⌒ *7th* ⌒

We were both inclined to be recluses. I more than you because you went out to do the shopping. Now I venture out into the world from my green bower of solitude. I want to in a way. I want to escape the house, even the garden. It is a strange house now, as if I have just moved in. I am numb today with the blow of sudden realisation. Sick . . .

It's funny, I remember you not as you were, but as you used to be.

I feel too weak to put the hoover on the house, and make do with desultory runs with the sweeper where it matters most. How grief withdraws energy, as the sap of a tree is drawn down to its roots in autumn, and the leaves wither! So in grief is all the energy of the body needed for its survival.

I conserve my remaining strength for the shopping expeditions I must now make. A long cycle ride to the bus. Then home to cats, goats, birds – all awaiting their midday feed before I can sit down to a cup of tea. After a rest unpacking the shopping and all the jobs.

You thought the disposal of the shopping a time-consuming task, but what about me with the animals and all the chores to tackle as well? No, no, I know it's not your fault. I would not grieve you – I want you to be happy.

In time I will be strong again. Robust. Full of vitality and the power of a positive mind.

── *8th* ──

One of my chief concerns has been fitting everything in so as not to neglect the feeding of the birds. How you tolerated my rituals. All those regular bird-table meal-times, on the dot, as if this were a restaurant and the birds the customers. I arranged the time of your funeral to suit their feeding time.

Your interest in the birds and their needs began that snowy winter morning when you opened the door on to a white garden and a whole flock of little birds – chaffinches, blue tits, great tits, robins – flew down to you, all crowding round the step. You were amazed and delighted. You picked up one of the cats and said, 'Here, look at this.'

Later you made the tall bird-table, and all the bird-boards to put high in the hedge. You brought fat home for them, big bagfuls, joked and cajoled out of the butcher.

You were always joking. Some people didn't understand. Those who did came to know and appreciate the real person that was you. You were unique, in your way.

── *9th* ──

I cannot find the postal order you bought for the football pool. It was with your bits and pieces when they brought the bag home to me. I was not going to continue with it – only this one, as you had prepared it, but thinking it over perhaps it is just as well it has disappeared. I would hate to win now, just me, when you wanted to so much.

It is no use people saying money isn't happiness, because in this world money and plenty of it is essential for civilised living, especially for the older generation.

But we had the miracle of the new bungalow to replace our old tumbledown one, didn't we? Thanks to Sam. For this last year you were able to sit and drink your tea in a comfortable armchair in a warm room, to go to bed in a snug bedroom, to have all the benefits of electricity instead of paraffin lamps. It was a good year. Thanks to Sam.

⟶ 10th ⟿

I shall have to make an effort of will to get out of this chair. I gaze and gaze at the space between the bottom of the settee and the carpet and think that if I could telescope my body I could crawl under it. Insects and small creatures do have an advantage. So many hiding places.

I have only just fully realised you are not coming back. It makes me feel sick inside, and lost, and so, so sad. The only thing to do is not to think of it like that. To think instead that you have gone out, and I shall be coming to meet you. Which I will when the time comes. It won't be too long. This is the last lap of my life on earth. I too will be free. You are free now of the bondage of time – you who always mourned the swiftness of the passing weeks.

One thing is certain – I must go on. I cannot go back. Tomorrow is nearer than yesterday because I know its pattern. The familiar pattern of yesterday is becoming remote, misty. Just like when the mist from the sea floats silently over the fields and cuts off all visibility, marooning our bungalow.

I am knitting again. Plodding along stitch by stitch like a heavy-footed pedestrian. How I used to skim along the needles, swift as a bicycle downhill!

Each day is a mountain to climb. A week is a whole range of mountains. They are only little mountains. They must be, because each night I reach the summit. However stiff the climb, last thing at night I can say, 'I made it.'

I never seemed to have enough time before, always trying to catch up with myself in a breathless race. Now there is a whole ocean of time.

It is hardest on days I don't go out. I think more. But I must think of the days ahead as a journey to meet you, a journey that will no doubt have its interests, as journeys do.

— 11th —

Sitting in the rocking chair in the doorway of the veranda, I rock gently in the sun. Have just had my dinner, only my second proper dinner for a fortnight.

I look out upon the green fields sloping to the skyline. One is empty now of sheep – only the house cow from the house at the top. She does not seem to mind there are no other cows. She never took any notice of the sheep, always grazing quietly by herself. Now she is really alone. Like me. But like her I am not a lonely person.

Presently she will be fetched home for milking, and will have company. But only human company. Not her own kind. She will not mind.

People come here. They are not you. But I must not mind either.

— 12th —

I picked up the small saucepan – not the smallest, the medium one. I wondered why it was so light. It was light because there were no potatoes in it. I had expected there to be potatoes in it because you always put them there. Ready.

— 17th —

Yes, I could weep sometimes now, long and softly, with the heart torn out of me, for all that we had and all that never was. Yet the never-was will come. In the circle of eternity all is held safe, and it is there waiting for us.

I had to walk over the pavement where you fell . . . where you died. It felt so strange, walking over the spot your body had covered for the few minutes before the ambulance arrived. Like walking on you. I couldn't do anything as conspicuous as placing flowers there, but I placed a thought. That you would be happy. You looked happy when they brought you home to me. That little lift to your mouth, like a smile. You laughed a lot at life, but in the battle you seldom smiled. Due, no doubt, to the art of the undertaker, you smiled in death.

Pavement flowers are not for you. For you the meadow-sweet in the hedge. Deep in the bright green grass where the hedge grows hazel and oak and beech that you cut for the goats – that is where you should have died. Perhaps I would have found you, and we could have shared your peace. There is no peace in a grey street, choking with people, belching traffic.

— *20th* —

Hudson misses you. Now you are not on the bed having your afternoon rest he doesn't go in there. He curls up on the settle in the dining room.

It was he who solved the problem of your pillow that first night.

I stood looking for some time at those two pillows side by side on the bed so companionably, and only one required. I wondered what to do. Anyone would have thought it was a major problem, the way I pondered it. Should I leave them there and sleep my side as usual? Should I remove yours? Take it right away? Should I put it underneath mine? Should I sleep in the middle of the bed? I was in an agony of indecision.

Hudson came in. He went straight to your pillow and curled up on it. As you know he has never done such a thing in his life. He has always slept at the foot of the bed.

He stayed on your pillow all night. The following night he slept at the bottom of the bed again. By then I had solved the problem. *Your* pillow goes under the bedclothes in the centre of the bed, and I lean against it, comforted.

I made the bed today, properly, for the first time since you went. Have just been falling into it and pulling the clothes over me. It seemed strange, making it again. The same sheets in which you slept. I shall have to change them, shan't I? . . . Wash away even the imprint of your body.

— *27th* —

We are so fragile, we the bereaved. We feel we may break into little pieces at any moment. We cannot stand against a breath of wind and hardly know how to put one foot in front of the other at times.

At dawn the day looms large and menacing, and if physical needs did not soon assert themselves we would probably cower under the bedclothes for hours. But if we proceed calmly, doing each thing that lies to our hand to do, we become aware of an inner propulsion, at first as if we have merely switched ourselves on and are moving and doing as automatons, but later we become aware that there is more life to it than that; the creative urge to live and be has sprung up like a little rooted plant from the divine seed of our origins.

March

— 7th —

There are times when I am wearied to the depths of my being with the world and daily life. Even as you were, in those deeply depressive moods. But I know I must not be. I must be positive and even joyful – joyful because of all the good things, because of the gift of life itself. I must regard the rest of my journey through the days as an adventure. I am going to live a very organised life. You would have approved of that.

It is lucky I am not a nervous person, living out here on my own with just the farm across the way. So much violence in the world today, but I feel quite safe. I remember, 'He that dwelleth in the secret place of the Most High . . . there shall no evil befall thee.'

The secret place . . . So far my nearest approach is God-consciousness. I cultivate this in my thinking and breathing. With a slow, deep breath you can draw in peace to your very soul.

⌒ *10th* ⌒

There was a whole flock of sheep in the garden when I got back from town. Quite a sight. Woolly shapes smothering the banks; muddy hooves churning up the grass.

They were easy to shift. As soon as I walked up behind them they streamed out of the garden and across our field in a body, coming to a standstill at the bank at the bottom where they had to squeeze under the fence in single file. But they all got through. I just had to watch to see none got entangled in the barbed wire or bramble.

The other day one was completely caught up in bramble, held fast by its wool in the spiky growth. It took some minutes to free it, and I had to do it wearing my gardening gloves.

What a good thing our gardens proper, yours and mine, are enclosed in fences because of the goats, or these sheep would ravage them.

I shall have to look after your garden now as well as mine. At the moment it makes me sad just to look at it. I remember your plans for the spring. Anyway, you achieved the winter cabbages. Just as you wished, the ground is covered in the well grown results of your labours.

It is certainly a good thing I have always managed the goats. I would be in a hole now if I couldn't do it. I can hump bales of hay and straw about almost as easily as you, and when the time comes to bury them a farmer will help me if necessary. You will be spared that.

Do you remember when we buried Frisky? He was the first of the goats to die. You wept over him, and kissed him. I tried to help you by telling you what I know to be true. 'He has another body,' I said. You replied angrily,

'Don't give me that!' You were angry because you would have liked to believe it, but couldn't. Now you *know*.

— 17th —

I go to town a different way to the way you went. Don't disapprove. I ride out to the main road on my bike. There is a safe place to leave it when I catch the bus.

Don't say I should go to the village and leave the bike at a house. I couldn't bear to sit in the village bus shelter thinking of you sitting there rolling your cigarettes . . .

Why do I feel so hollowed out inside like a Hallowe'en lantern without a light, when I know that you have gone into a happiness such as you have never known? Why am I not lit with joy for you, since your happiness was always my desire? I am sad, sad, sad because you are gone and I am bound and tethered, stranded in a limbo between two worlds. Yours I cannot enter; mine has grown dark.

— 19th —

It is Sunday evening. I cannot switch on *Songs of Praise* on the television, because you always did – not because you believed, but because you were seeking. Always seeking. Seeking, but not finding. I had already found some of the treasure, but we could not share it because you were always that one step behind. Now you are one step ahead of me.

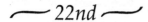

— 22nd —

I am a completely free being. I can come and go as I please. I can do as I like. I have no one to consider. It is all 'I'. I am like Dinky in the big birdcage years ago after his partner Dandy had died. He had the freedom of the cage. How he revelled in it! How he sang! His head-feathers stood on end and he sang at the top of his voice. I cannot sing, but I know the feeling.

And I would give it all up to see you walk again through that door.

— 24th —

I think you were with me in the butcher's today. I dreaded going in there – four serving, and I must buttonhole the one you always dealt with because I want only animal food, and he knows exactly what to weigh up, and is generous.

I must stand with customers who will spend so much more than my £1.20, choosing their cuts of meat with critical appraisal, thinking nothing of changing their minds and rejecting one for another, and receiving deferential treatment because they have *money*.

I don't eat meat and should not be there at all, but I cannot deprive the cats of their liver. It is so stupid to feel humble and embarrassed – stupid, ridiculous, and unnecessary.

You seem to tell me to take it more lightly. When the wrong butcher approaches me, instead of stammering awkwardly I find myself saying brightly, 'I'm waiting for this young man.' This is not me. This is you. And when he says jokingly, 'Him? He's not a young man,' I actually quip, 'He's young enough for me.'

The moment passes lightly. I feel pleased and proud of myself, and close to you. It was the way you always sailed through situations. There was wisdom behind your jokes.

— 25th —

How sensitive grief makes you to the things people say or do not say. Beware the bereaved. Those who walk with them must walk on egg shells. Only true love in the heart can prevent unintentional hurt.

We who are bemused by grief walk a strange path. The familiar becomes unfamiliar, the plain places rough. We see everything in infinitesimal detail as if something in us stands separate from our everyday eyes, engaged solely in dispassionate observation. We register the flight of a bird as if we had never seen it before, pictures on walls, newspaper headlines, the grey splashing of grey rain on the wet shine of a grey street.

I write down words. They come from inside me, not of my own volition. I must write them. I, who thought I would never write again. I have continually to leave what I am doing to come and write them down. Peeling an onion, I have to drop the knife for a pen. Perversely, I write at the back of a bound foolscap book – one of yours – writing from back to front, very small, as if I do not really want the words to see the light of day.

— 28th —

The days now are passing at the cracking pace of a high-speed train. At first they dragged, but now they whirl me along, always depositing me within the next twenty-four hours.

How the passing of time frightened you. The week merging into another so swiftly. You did not seem to have time to live and you did not, as I do, know that life is for ever, that we really live in eternity, where there is no time at all.

 *30th*

Let neither of us grieve over the things that were wrong. No regrets. What was undone must still be done, the unfinished finished, the mistakes rectified. Life will bring us full circle till all is accomplished. Life – the continuity of life – takes care of everything. You know that now.

I know you are free – free of the burden of the physical body and its limitations, free of the labour of life on earth. Free and happy in your spiritual body on a higher plane where Truth manifests. So, knowing you are transported to great happiness and even watching over me to help, why should I be sad?

I substitute the desire for your physical presence by concentrating on constructing the enjoyment of *little* things. A perilous edifice at first if I too feverishly seek to build it up. If I let the moments come naturally I am safe.

The secret is to take nothing for granted. I must actively enjoy the apparently ordinary, which means living consciously all the time, completely absorbed in each moment.

I consciously sip a cup of tea, relishing its warmth and flavour, enjoy the comfort of dry clothes after a douche of rain, appreciate the affection of a purring cat, enjoy the comfortable sound of goats munching, eat my little bit of food slowly, seeking the individual taste of each ingredient.

The day is not a stretch of hours. It is constructed of moments, and in each moment I try to live in awareness not of its emptiness because you are not here but of the fullness of the moment itself and what is happening within it.

April

1st

The spring brings me no solace, no message – perhaps because I do not need one. I never cared for this season of the year, anyway. It arouses no poetic feelings in me. I am too aware of the starker reality, the mixture as before. It is too close to the brutality of winter. The young lambs, born for slaughter and roast dinners, are more likely to suffer hardship in their brief lives than to spend them in halcyon days, crying in the onslaught of fierce winds and ice-tipped rain more often than frolicking in the warmth of the sun. The daffodils bow and bend and break, the tender leaf-buds of the horse chestnut rush out too soon and are bruised black and brown around their edges, rain-water pours off the fields in rivers and thick, squelchy mud spreads like clotted cream vomited.

I prefer autumn with its aura of tranquillity before the winter gales set in, its sense of things satisfyingly accomplished. Even as your earth life has been accomplished.

— 3rd —

I thought the hollow sick feeling had gone, but today it assailed me again for no apparent reason as I steadily progressed through the day. I was even pleased with my achievements. What brought it about? Nothing really. A repercussion from my subconscious, reminding me, as I must so often have informed it in the early days, that I now travel alone.

So I liken it to travel sickness. And that can be alleviated, if not cured. I must find a resting place on the journey today. A place of peace for ailing travellers. Peace is the antidote. The kind of peace that flows through your whole being like a river in flood.

A single sentence, painstakingly repeated (silently, in the mind) innumerable times to quieten turbulent thoughts is usually the way I find it. When it absorbs my whole attention, my complete awareness, becoming as it were part of my very self, in heart and bloodstream, then I find the place of peace to rest in for a while.

What sentence shall I choose today? It could be almost anything that could focus the attention in a meaningful way as the gentle, relaxed repetition of it continues. Perhaps today it will be, 'Lo, I am with you always, even unto the end of the world.'

— 8th —

I have this vague anxiety, this tendency to unrest. Peace will quell it, oceans of peaceful breathing and thinking in which I submerge myself as a relaxed bather in a gentle sea. Quell but not cure. I cannot find the root of the trouble, to wrest it out.

Yesterday I weeded under the rose hedge where young stinging nettles were congregating again, and their roots came out by the metre – long, tough, endless strings of root that eventually broke, and if even a small piece remains it will again send up a nettle to grow where it should not. I could not get every bit of root out, so later there will be battle to be waged again. I hate this destruction. To keep a garden one must be aggressive and destructive, and I cannot reconcile this with the creativity of gardening.

Anyway, my hidden anxiety is springing from a root within with the characteristics of the roots of the stinging nettle. Awareness and fear of being 'alone in the world' – is that the cause? Something my conscious mind rejects because I am not really alone. Outside in the world I have friends. People I can turn to if need be, knowing they will help.

Of course there is nothing to fear. In every problem, every difficulty, I have drawn upon that well of inner wisdom that lies deep within the human psyche, and each time I have come through unscathed.

Little by little I must root out the unwanted and unnecessary anxiety by sending down into my subconscious the reassurance of positive thoughts. I want to think strongly, positively, constructively, to bring benefit not only to myself but to others. Thought is a power.

9th

I think you came to visit us today – 'us' being the house, the cats and me. It was Hudson who saw you. Just as I put his food down he looked up sharply from his plate towards the porch door, then turned tail to flee to the bathroom like he always does when someone calls. I went to look, but there was nobody there.

'It's all right, Hudson,' I said. 'Nobody there.' He had already stopped in his tracks, looking back, and now stood staring up at what to me was space. He saw something – someone. He stared and stared at the invisible.

Later I was sitting in the dining-room, very quiet and concentrated, thinking. There was a loud knock, apparently at the veranda door. I went at once. Nobody. No cat. No goat. No wind. Nothing.

I expect you do come sometimes. I have never thought of it, never waited, listened, wondered. I always think of you as being on holiday in a far country to which I too shall be travelling when I have done all the packing up here.

How fortunate you are to have reached the next stage of life. We in this world are all like ants on an anthill, endlessly labouring for survival.

As each shopping day comes round I go to the same shops and buy the same things in order to stay alive, revolving in an endless circle of survival. How you understood the feeling – how you revolted against the trivialities, the repetitiveness of daily life. You could never come to terms with it; you knew that life should be so much more than this, something free and poetic and liberating . . . The shackles hurt so much because you did not know that one day, in casting them off, you would enter into Life Itself where there are no numbered days, no trivialities, no restrictions, no battles for survival, but only an ecstasy of living.

Of course, this narrow view of life in the world is entirely the wrong attitude. I am digging a pit for myself and falling into it. I should be climbing the hillside under an open sky to the wider view at the top.

— *12th* —

I have decided to go along with life. Whatever has happened, whatever happens. To cut out fretting, fuming, pondering, repetitive remembering, 'kicking against the pricks'. I will just *go along*.

What a sense of freedom this gives as it gets through to my consciousness. Freedom, light-heartedness, peace, wholeness, satisfaction, well-being. You are gone. Right. I accept it. If it rains, it rains. I go out in it regardless.

This is not resignation. It is going on. Travelling on. I cope, I tackle, I overcome, I enjoy, I live Life Itself. This is a personal thing. No one else can live life for me. Partnered or alone, I *live*. Life is to be *lived*. Life is not repining. One breathes and *lives*. It is an awareness, a *being*. It is Today. So tomorrow will be a repetition of today. That doesn't matter. Tomorrow isn't life. Each day is the day when life is *lived*. For that matter even repetition can be cancelled out by the power to think. It is all an attitude of mind. By thinking I change things.

— *13th* —

Joy is the secret of life. The realisation of *being* – I am. At the first impact of this realisation there is an onrush of joy as if from a hidden source deep within. Life is living. Living is being. Being is *I am*.

Everything becomes magical. Breathing, moving, resting, seeing, knowing. You do not need another person's presence to live in this sense. You are complete because you suddenly become aware of one-ness, of being part of a whole. The whole Universe. And that embraces people known and unknown and every part of Creation.

That is the top of the mountain. To live always in this rarefied state is not possible, at least in the early stages. Descending, how easy it is to forget . . .

I find it helps to talk. I don't mean to others – when I am alone at home I not only talk to the cats, but to myself, to cheer myself along. It's only like thinking aloud. There's nothing crazy about it. I like to use my voice and to hear the sound of it, and there is satisfaction in it as I tell myself what I am going to do next, what the weather is, how I feel, my plans and aims, etc., etc., *ad infinitum*.

I remember an old lady who lived in Bournemouth many years ago when I was a child. We were on holiday and booked with her for bed and breakfast. It was a little house, and she pottered around in it in slip-slop slippers. She talked to herself too. Her favourite remarks concerned her household tasks. 'That's that,' she would say comfortably, 'and this is this.' She was a placid little person and her little house was friendly as if it absorbed an atmosphere from her unhurried movements and peaceful soliloquys.

⌒ *18th* ⌒

I so often 'see' you going in and out. Passing through the kitchen, saying, 'All right, then?' I slit a leek and hear you say, 'Mind how you go with that knife.' I get ready to go out in the rain and hear you say, 'We can't have you going out in this. I'll get your pension when I go out tomorrow.' But you will not be here tomorrow.

I could have wept today for very weariness. Weariness of the plodding hours, of work, work, work. I must work all the time even now with all my good intentions or I am a prey to sorrow that will creep up on me like an insidious serpent from under my mind. I know I must use my mind to control it, as all wayward creatures must be controlled. My mind is my own. It is my own computer. I can tell it what to think. It doesn't have to think about sorrow. If I cannot bring myself to inspire it with high thoughts, I think mundane ones. What I will do tomorrow. A shopping list. Plan, plan, plan. I can always make small plans. They, after all, are the map of my journey through the days. Without a map you lose your way. If I panic I think, 'I must proceed calmly.' And I continue as if nothing had happened, as if everything is normal, and let the moments absorb me in the doing of things.

Some days are very strange. I do battle with myself all morning and in the afternoon there is a kind of tranquillity. Physical effort, like cycling, brings tranquillity. I ask myself, 'Is this the same day?' and again, 'Am I the same person?'

Outside the window a blue spring sky is crowded with big white clouds. There was a bookmark in my library book. It was rather nice, so I handed it in as someone might ask for it. 'I wandered lonely as a cloud' was printed on it. For the first time since learning, reading, remembering and coming across that line it occurred to me that a cloud is seldom lonely. How often does one see a solitary cloud? They crowd together, like the daffodils.

⌒ *25th* ⌒

I have found a way to combat sudden panic, anxiety, fretting or frustration. Very firmly I tell myself, 'I *can* cope. I *am* coping', and then take the next task to hand.

To endeavour to grasp the ideas or truths hidden in words that could be taken as meaningless or beyond comprehension is a good exercise for a troubled or turbulent mind. It gives the mind occupation, and soothes it as more peaceful feelings take over. I am trying this out, at the moment meditating, turning the words over and over, wondering, pondering – call it what you will – on 'The kingdom of heaven is within you'. Taken as a fact it is incredibly exciting, opening up a great new vista into invisible mysteries.

Since thinking it over, other words occurred to me – somewhere it says that the kingdom of heaven is taken by violence. 'The violent take it by force,' as I remember the words. Linked with 'The kingdom of heaven is within you', a meaning emerges. Strong desire and great emotion can batter an *inner* fortress – and suddenly you are 'there'. Where? Well, didn't it happen to me once? I never told you. It was impossible to share it then. A moment of unbelievable distress tearing me apart inside brought about an unforgettable spiritual experience. It was real and true because it transformed my life from that time on.

28th

Outside the window of the little room the budding branches of the sycamore sway in the east wind. I look up through the twiggy black boughs, through a haze of pale green to the blue spring sky. Higher up the buds are pearly in the sun. Watching the movement of the branches is hypnotic. I am almost in the tree, part of it.

Such moments make the day worthwhile – and I only came in here to drink a cup of coffee between jobs.

May

9th

I am pottering through the day today.

An old love, pottering. It is nice to go back to it. I never pottered when you were here.

Today I had little choice. I meant to go shopping but the east wind drove me indoors. Bad enough feeding the birds in it, but I was *not* going out on the bike. It would have to be an indoor day except for looking after the animals. I could do important housewifely things like hoovering, but the hoover scares Hudson out of his wits so I always do it when he is in the garden. He couldn't stay out there today so I salved my housewifely conscience by doing some washing, and then I pottered. I wrote half a letter, drank coffee, scribbled, sat in the sun by the window, and did a lot of little things of no importance at all.

10th

I must stop seeing the rest of my life as a weary routine of days. It's like travelling in a train with the blinds down, and it gives me such a heavy, bogged-down feeling. I want to see Life – pulsating, breathing Life – as a *wonder*; a fresh wonder every day. I want to realise that Life is a living thing totally unrelated to mere daily survival; to experience it flowing in my veins and bringing me *joy*.

True joy is in no way related to circumstances, outward events, or anyone other than the individual experiencing it – that is, it is not dependent upon someone else (you) being there. It is entirely personal, welling up from realisation of its presence within. An expansion of consciousness, perhaps. The whole point is there is no *outward* cause. Joy flows from Life Itself. If only it were possible to live all the time on so high a plane. I have been there.

It's a wonderful discovery when pure joy is experienced, untouched by adverse circumstances. Simply welling up from within. Yet it is not I who generated it. The 'within' is a holy place of which I know almost nothing, except that it is not confined to the physical boundaries of my earthly body. It is linked to the Universe, to the Source of all Joy, to Life Itself – Life, that invisible spark or essence or spirit that animates all things

— *11th* —

I am becoming more and more aware of the unseen aspect of Life. Pushing the bike uphill, I thought of the roots of the hedgerow; the strength of the roots hidden deep in the rich leaf-fed soil. I thought of the vitality of grass, the radiant health of flowers manifesting in the untarnished gold of the gorse, the wide-awake primroses, the clustered violets in a crowd of blue. All these along the lane's edge.

I did more than think – I drew deep of all this strength, vitality and health flowing from an unseen source, and incredibly I no longer found the way wearisome as I usually do, pushing uphill home. Instead I covered the distance in half the time without once pausing to rest. I marvelled; the propulsion had been the power of my concentrated and directed thought.

— 15th —

You are on a different wavelength now. That is why you have vanished as far as this world is concerned. Just as one picture gives way to another when the television channel is changed. Where you are now is where we came from, our source – our real home. You live in a replica of the body I buried, fashioned in the same material as the plane you now inhabit. Certainly not of the earth, earthy. The physical has gone, but you are still you. Your world is invisible to us because of the different dimension. *That's all it is*.

The insects and little creatures in the world of the hedgerow do not see anything of the lives of the humans above them. If *we* could actually *see* into *your* world we would find it impossible to live in this one for the wonder and the joy of it.

— 19th —

I find pleasure in little things. The small bunches of greenery gathered on the way home for the goats' supper treat. Tiny treasures of young sycamore leaves, hawthorn and blackthorn sprigs, sprays of honeysuckle leaves. All carefully garnered on their short twigs from the close-cut hedges. Presently there will be an abundance of growth, and then I shall gather branches, but that will not give me the same exquisite pleasure these tiny bunches give.

Then the pleasure of dunking a ginger biscuit in a cup of decaffeinated coffee. Even of apportioning the pension money to cover the necessities. Nothing over this week, but everything covered.

— 21st —

I am over the phase of remembering when you were here – still physically around, likely to come in at any moment. Now I wonder if you were ever here at all.

Has it always been like this – just me? The tangible evidence is there – your coat hanging in the porch, your cup still at the back of the draining board, near the kettle. Awaiting the next tea-making. But these things no longer mean anything. They do not speak to me of you as they did at first. Before, your absence was the dream. Now your being here – once – is like something I dreamed.

But you lived here, once. The clippers are in the pocket of your coat. You used them to cut sprigs from the hedges for the goats. I come in the gate – it is your gate – the gate you made so carefully to the cat specifications. Their little cat houses stand beyond the door-step – you made those too because they sometimes like to sit in the fresh air when it's raining. The caravan is yours, full of your books and tools. It is all evidence that you lived here – so why do I feel that you have never been here at all, that it has always been like this, just me and the cats and the house?

The whole world is a dream because nothing in it is permanent. Only the real is permanent, and there is nothing permanent here. Everything here will pass from its material existence as if it had never been.

You have awakened from the dream and entered Reality. So, one day, will I.

— 22nd —

It is dangerous to live beyond the day. The sixteen hours of total occupation, of physical labour, of mental absorption in book or writing or television images make a safe enclosed space, like a walled garden, beyond which lies the turmoil of the streets. Tomorrow, next week, next month, next year, the next ten years do not intrude, just as the traffic does not violate a garden. By the seventeenth hour, if I have been busy enough and tired myself out, I am fast asleep in dreamless peace, merely to waken only partially now and then to turn over and sleep again.

To live beyond the day is to enter dangerous territory, where every step leads to a chasm or a bog or ways that are steep and stony, and nothing is visible in a semi-darkness where terror lurks. So I stay safely within the day.

— 23rd —

The chestnut tree is in mourning for you. Every year, as you know, it is in such a hurry to greet the spring that its tender young leaves rush out in March, a delicate green crowd as eager to burst from their big brown buds as children pouring out of school. And every year the weather is violent to them, betraying their simple trust in finding soft air and sunshine and sweet, gentle showers.

The wise old ash knows this and holds back its leaves until all possible danger is past. It has never yet been caught out, but the chestnut tree always suffers.

This year it was worse than usual. A bitter salt-laden gale off the sea, raging at high pitch for days on end, pitilessly sapped the life-energy of the little leaves.

Now, in May, each hangs from its twig like a torn brown ribbon.

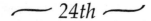 *24th*

Your birthday. You didn't like birthdays, did you? Nevertheless I hugged your coat hanging up in the porch and wished you a happy one. Because I know that *now* it will be. Remembering it, you will be glad you were born, that you have life.

June

7th

They all came down on holiday as usual. How you would have enjoyed the outings and conversation. We went to where your earthly body is, taking flowers. The pansies I planted there at Easter were still blooming, nestling into the turf of the mound.

They said goodbye to you when they came away. How could I truly reassure them that you are not there? They reach out after understanding and hope and try to believe, but they do not *know* as I know. I didn't say goodbye to you because I knew you were not there. Unless you were standing beside us, as you might well have been. *That* may be but a guess, a fancy, but the great true fact remains for ever – you are *alive*. We shall see you again.

That last evening, after they had gone, I realised significantly, for the first time in a clear-cut unalterable way, how alone I am. I felt alone in a way I have not felt before. No matter how independent one is, nor how much one likes doing one's own thing, the joy of sharing is precious. I shall have to double, redouble and treble my busyness.

I do not speak to anyone for three days at a time. This does not bother me. We both always enjoyed solitude, didn't we? I talk to myself and the animals, and on the fourth day, which is a shopping day, I say 'Thank you' in the supermarket.

We were a bit like Jack Sprat and his wife, only in a different way. You liked your dinner early; I liked my dinner late. You liked to go to bed early and get up in the night. I liked to go to bed late and sleep till morning.

How thankful I am that we did not live too close and inseparable. The complete solitariness now would be unendurable.

— 9th —

A woman in the shop said sympathetically to another, 'You're on your own now then?' She, grey-haired and stout, replied, 'Yes. He died last autumn.' To further commiserations she said, almost dismissively, 'Well, it happens. I'm not the only one. There are plenty of others.'

There are plenty of others. Of course. Bereavement is so isolated, so intimate, so a one-person experience that usually we, the bereaved, tend to live as islands in a sea of people living normal, everyday unmutilated lives. But to think of 'the others' – the others who, like ourselves, have a hole in their lives – is like finding oneself on a bridge no longer cut off.

Suddenly we are not islands, but a whole continent. A continent of people experiencing the same grief, striving for the same adjustment. Just to think of them links us all together. We are not alone any more. And if, in struggling for our own survival, a thought goes out, a strong, linking thought, maybe someone, somewhere, is sustained.

— *10th* —

I have a new, wonderful happiness. All out of nowhere, as it were. It is because I have entered a magic world, as if I were a child again. A world of wonder, where all is simple and believable and safe.

To outgrow such a world is perhaps childhood's biggest loss – not at first when the outside world becomes a kaleidoscope of romance and adventure, but later, in the warp and woof of life when the world is tarnished and the circumstances of life ordinary, when romance is lost in tedium and adventure in routine, and imagination no longer supplies an escape route.

We grow up unaware of 'the kingdom of heaven within' which we must become 'as little children' to enter. But once become aware of it . . .

This is the only Reality, this consciousness of the Power behind the universe. I reach out in my mind. I marvel with my thoughts. My heart is uplifted. Life Itself, continuous, creative Life, thrills through my physical body. I seek, I find, I *know*. Such knowing is the pearl of great price. I would not trade it for anything.

— *11th* —

I began this last stage of my life's journey with no desires at all, except to survive and look after the animals. Inside I was empty, like a kettle that has boiled dry. Now desires are germinating again. I will encourage them to flourish and will fulfil them all.

I am filled with expectancy – thrilled, as if wonderful things are awaiting me, like coming to a bend in a country lane and anticipating what may lie beyond it. Always something else round the next bend. Oh yes, it may be just the continuation of the road, and then another bend, and another and another, but always there is the possibility of something different, something special, something heart-lifting.

Anticipation opens the eyes so that you do not miss even the smallest thing. And I have such plans now, such ideas . . . I want to go through these scribblings, get them in some sort of order. Perhaps a book in your memory? You who loved books . . . There are so many – Thoreau, Edward Thomas, Richard Jefferies, W. H. Hudson, Joseph Conrad, Richard Aldington, Somerset Maugham, Raymond Chandler . . . I have been sorting them out.

⌐ *12th* ⌐

Even with my new desires I am still finding that I have to live within the moment, within a plan for the rest of the day, for tomorrow – but not beyond. Otherwise my ideas come up against a blank wall because you will not be there. A wall shutting me in with the past, with you again coming in and out the doors of the house, you who were always there when I needed you, you with whom I shared things.

When I am not concentrating upon the moment, not doing and planning more doing, it is then that I know for sure that you are gone. So my new ideas come to grief in that gulf of blankness.

I stand at the window and look across the deep fields of June and remember last year . . . It occurs to me that, like the year and the planet, the whole of life is a circle. There is no straight, untrodden course. We simply go round and round, experiencing the same things over and over . . . the same events, the same emotions, the same ideals, the same regrets, the same ambitions.

But it is not a roundabout. More like a multistorey car park. We are going somewhere, and if we keep going we reach the top.

I look across the green ocean of fields, and gradually my heart lifts.

⌒ 13th ⌒

Mornings are still chilly. I sat in the rocking chair in the veranda doorway before the sun was up with my cup of tea to enjoy the outside and to have the comfort of indoors simultaneously. I felt buoyant in the chair, stimulated by the freshness of the air, staring at the vast grey-blue sky spanning the summer fields and felt as if I could take off suddenly like a balloon. Rising up and up into the cloud cushions, floating above the oatmeal specks of sheep on the hillside.

I often used to think how pleasant it would be to float through the air under one's own steam, not mechanically propelled, not with wings, but just floating effortlessly. I bet you can do that now in the higher spheres.

⌒ 15th ⌒

My birthday – sixty-five! Imagine it. Me! Sixty-five! I remember once saying to someone, 'I don't feel any age at all.' And she replied matter-of-factly, 'Until you look in the mirror.' At which I laughed and said, 'I don't often do that.' Which was true. I only ever glance in it to pile up my hair, as you know. I haven't even powdered my nose since I was sixteen. And you always did prefer a fresh complexion to the porcelain look of make-up, just as I do.

So now I'm sixty-five and you would have been seventy-three. I cannot believe that, either. I suppose it is because I never thought of us as bodies. People always think of people as bodies unless, in companionship, the hidden truth comes through . . . that the *real* person is inside. The body inevitably shows signs of age, but the person inside is ageless.

⌐ *16th* ⌐

I do all the things I have to do, all the things that interest me. I eat, sleep, go out, come back, think creative thoughts, try to be positive . . . and yet underneath . . . underneath there is emptiness. I am empty, the house is empty, the whole overcrowded universe is empty . . .

⌐ *24th* ⌐

I discovered today – or rediscovered – how to avoid a day being melancholy, as some days are. You simply ignore its existence – more precisely, become unaware of it as a day, one of many.

It is like the hill, the steep hill I push my bike up to go to the village. I have always found that hill difficult, taking my breath, putting an ache behind my knees. I used to pause at least three times. Then, when the hedge growth grew, I went more slowly, breaking off bits of beech and oak for the goats as I went. I became absorbed in this, going slowly, selecting the best bits. Without being aware of it I came to the top of the hill as comfortably as if I had walked gently on level ground. I stood at the top and gazed down at the house nestling among the trees.

I knew then that I could conquer the day in the same way I had conquered the hill. It takes only absorption – complete absorption in the doing of things, and not thinking of the day at all, not thinking of it as hours, as morning, afternoon, evening, night. Just living within it, occupied and preoccupied with the doing of things.

July

I have failed in my own philosophy, the philosophy of the basic essential of absolute truth in all things, always. Like Hilaire Belloc,

> I said to heart, 'How goes it?'
> Heart replied,
> 'Right as a Ribstone pippin.'
> But it lied.

Yes, it lied. For I am sick. Sick of everything. Sick of being me. Sick of doing, sick of thinking, reading, looking, trying, planning. Sick of the drudgery of shopping, sick of cycling, sick of walking, sick of getting up, sick of the world's news. I am sick and weary to the centre of my soul of daily life in this world.

Right! That's it then. That's got that said and out into the open. So now let's get it into perspective. And isn't it a fact that most people have phases of the same weariness from time to time, letting things really get to them, whatever their circumstances? Yes, it is. You can have the happiest life imaginable and things can still get you down in the repetitiveness of daily life. The highs, the lows . . . the top of the mountain, the shadowed valley . . . and the little petty trickle of triviality running through the middle of everything.

So I will accept that for the moment it is all too much, and I will rest and relax and let it all go from me, and draw upon the deep *feeding* breath of Life Itself – great, infinite Life, pervading all things. Breathe deeply, drink deeply of the inhaled Breath and feel the thrill of response in the body, know the peace of it in the heart . . .

⟶ *13th* ⟶

The chestnut tree has shed its mourning and is again clad for summer. All those wind-burnt leaves shrivelled and died and dropped to make an autumn path in May. Miraculously since then more new young leaves have grown.

Last time spring leaves were lost, less drastically, the tree remained partly bare all summer. Now it is bright, light green with newness again, not a single leaf missing.

The wise tree, the ash, is also in full untarnished plumage. It held its leaves back later than ever this year till the last of the bitter, rampaging winds left the remaining weeks of spring to softer temperatures. The sprays of ash leaves, eleven to a stem, sway on supple boughs, each slim bough a great, green bouquet.

Ash, chestnut, sycamore, fir and my beloved withy tree by the house – of all these garden trees I think perhaps the ash is the loveliest. How trees soothe me, though – all of them.

— 20th —

I talk to animals, plants, inanimate objects. The sound of my voice brings a more comfortable, everyday feeling into the atmosphere of the house, bereft of your presence, and even at times into the great outdoors stretching into an infinity of sky. At those times I need companionship rather than contemplation. For of course I have always loved being alone among fields and trees and sky and absorbing *their* atmosphere. But sometimes now that expanse of fields makes me feel lonely, as if I am lost in an empty desert, as if the world is too big for me. But the trees are always friendly and comforting.

I once told someone that I talked to things. 'But you never get any answers,' she said with sympathy. Somehow the answers don't really matter. It's the sound of my voice in the silence that is the helpful aspect of this eccentricity.

The cats answer me, anyway, especially Hudson. You know well enough the range of *his* conversational powers. I know every flexible nuance, and smile over the translation. The goats answer me too. I love their voices, whether it is a murmur or a bawl.

I talk to my bike when I'm riding it, but that began long ago as a child riding along a country lane to school. The bike had a name, and I rode it as if it were a horse. Today the firmness of the handlebars under my fingers, the springy saddle, and the whirr of the wheels make me feel I am out with a friend.

I have personalised the two bikes I have now. (Forgot to tell you recently that I bought another bike, a second-hand one, to make sure I always have immediate transport should one get a puncture.)

I feel a strong affinity with those two bikes, for in a way

they are my lifeline. The shopping is absolutely dependent upon them, and also any excursions I wish to make. There is something very companionable too about a bike when riding it.

I remembered the Bikel of childhood, and decided to name these. But what can you sensibly name a bike? Fleet, Swift, Streak? More likely Plodder on these inclines and hills! But the clue was there, for each already actually had a name. There they were, boldly printed on the cross-bar – Revelation and Cosmopolitan. So now they are Revel and Cosmo, and I can urge them along by name to inspire myself to further pedal effort as I go along. 'Come on, Revel, up you go . . .'; 'Let it zip, Cosmo, fast as you can . . .' Revel, encumbered with the big cat-basket in the front in which I pack half the shopping – the rest on the carrier. Cosmo, delightfully winged of wheel without extra weight is for the village and trips around the lanes. Cosmo is a real goer – we zoom along.

⌒ 31st ⌒

I have reached a point where there is too much activity in my life. I no longer need to feverishly fill each hour with physical movement or concentrated mental effort in order to keep the realisation of your absence at bay. No longer need I fear to know realistically that you will not walk through the door. I *do* know you live; I *do* sense your presence at times.

Now I can accept the change because a new phase is opening in my life. My spiritual awareness is increasing. Much as I have sought it before, gained a little, lost it in the turmoil of living, aloneness is the only atmosphere in which it can more fully open. I have that circumstance now, and I have denied it by continuous activity. I have been like a bee, here, there, everywhere, endlessly working, always on the move. Sitting only to eat, to read, never to think except to plan the next move, the next meal, the next shopping list, the next jobs to do; even falling asleep at night reading.

Now I can sit quietly relaxed in the rocking chair watching through the glass door the scatter of sheep in the field opposite, feeling a new peace, reaching out for deeper understanding. Feeling all the *hidden* things in the universe, the unknown wonder; knowing there is a deep well of wisdom waiting to be drawn upon, to yield its secrets to the searching heart. I have run hard; now I can pause and find refreshment.

I am cultivating a great calm like an immense sunlit sea. Yet at the same time I feel an aliveness, a buoyancy, as if my sea has a gentle ripple of little waves. It's a lovely feeling.

August

1st

Hot summer days. A real old-fashioned summer, reminiscent of bare-legged childhood in the cool freedom of woods, of stifling office days. How glad you must be to have missed it. Last year you were so thankful it was not hot for the shopping. Now it is I who am encumbered with it – but oh! I'm so glad it is not you. You who became so weary of everyday life, of weather and toil.

I wear little, and hoist my rucksack, smaller than yours but heavy with vegetables and tins of cat food, only temporarily on to my back in the baking street, then sweat in the bus to where the bike is parked – Revel, of course, because of the big basket on the front – and there, thankfully, unload, distributing the weight between basket and carrier.

Revel takes all the weight. I ride unaware of it, with only the journey itself to negotiate – the long incline home, first along the main road in the roaring stream of holiday traffic with a breeze to refresh me, then into the pitiless heat of the lane where the sun's temperature is trapped between high hedges until I reach the cool canopy of the woods.

I know you watch and share this marathon. I am not alone.

— 2nd —

I sit in the rocking chair in the veranda doorway, drinking my morning coffee and watching the tall brown grasses in the field sway in the light wind that drifts refreshingly into the heat, the white butterflies endlessly flitting above them.

I have seen only two coloured butterflies this year. One a peacock. The other was gone too swiftly to identify. All the chrysalises we left suspended at the top of the veranda walls perished in the winter. Not for either of us the pleasure of capturing the moment when a butterfly emerged brand new on a summer morning.

How valiantly those little caterpillars worked to find themselves a suitable position last autumn. Such a long trek across the concrete path from the garden, and then the apparently endless climb, first up the short wall and then up the wall of the veranda itself until they reached the ceiling. Sometimes I watched them – remember coming out to look?

When we later pointed out the chrysalises to D, all suspended there, to us embryo-butterflies, to her debris blown in from the garden, 'I would have swept those down,' she said. We might as well have done so, since their marathon was in vain. But they had their chance. In the cycle of life they will probably have another chance, another year.

⟋ *3rd* ⟍

What a funny life . . . What-a-funny-life . . . I sit in the
rocking chair and rock. Time divided into day and
night . . . day after day after day . . . night after night
after night . . . a circle of repetitive days and nights. What
a funny life . . . I rock and rock and rock . . .

You knew this feeling. Perhaps it's why people climb
mountains and do other adventurous things. Me, I rock
and ponder, ponder and rock, until I regain a little sanity
and find again the upward path that leads out of this
circular tour of days and nights.

⟋ *4th* ⟍

It's a butterfly summer. Pity there aren't more butterflies
to enjoy it. Just this sprinkling of whites, flitting and flirt-
ing in the field (when they aren't visiting the cabbages).

I remember once walking up the sun-trapped turning
of the lane in a whole procession of flitting butterflies of
all colours. And where are the bees? Not one zooms by.
The harmony of humming we heard summers ago, so
tranquillising, is no more.

There is a wasps' nest in one of the sheds. They seem
happy enough. I shall leave it there.

You would have done that too. You who picked up all
the baby crabs high up on the shore of the estuary that
day they were cast out of the salmon nets, and returned
them to the sea because you were aware that it distressed
me to see them stranded. Just as you turned me sharply
away when they were puncturing the ears of the cattle at
the cattle market, so sorry that you had taken me there.
These are the little memories that return now, with

warmth rather than sadness. They remind me so vividly of *you*. I think I will start a notebook of all the *nice* memories. It will while away a hot afternoon and help me to think of you constructively.

⌒ *6th* ⌒

Wish you were here. I have to take Magpie to the vet tomorrow. I miss not being able to share the slight anxiety with you. She was so wet when she washed herself that it led me to discover her very wet mouth. The dribble may be gum or tooth trouble. If it means tooth extraction I am hoping so much that she won't have to stay in. The rest of it is bad enough for her – the five-mile journey in the basket on the bike, the wait when we arrive, the vet's table . . . Thinking of such things used to put me in a minor panic, but I am succeeding in mastering myself.

Today being Sunday I would have found it hard to get through, unable to take her till tomorrow, but now I have a beautiful calm. I would still like to share this with you, though. Yet it would have been me comforting you when it came to the point. 'She'll be all right, won't she?' you'd say. And I would reply, 'Yes, of course she will.' So I will say it to you now just the same – she'll be all right.

⌒ *7th* ⌒

Magpie is safe home. She has had five teeth out, but doesn't seem aware of the fact. I took her in this morning and fetched her this afternoon.

How pleased you would have been to see her arrive back, and come out of the basket. It was a pleasure I had to enjoy by myself.

I was so tired out with travel and anxiety I took her on to the bed and we had a lie down together, she still dopey from the anaesthetic. She snuggled, purring. There was a period of beautiful, restful calm and sweet drifting into a state of dreaming half-sleep, listening to the bliss of her purr. This was the happiest couple of hours I have had since you went.

— 10th —

I have got to find a way to live that will satisfy and fulfil me. There is satisfaction in doing things, even in the successful accomplishment of certain everyday things, but beyond that – nothing.

If I could live within my mind all the time, in the secret inner place, where directed thought uplifts me, all would be a balanced, harmonious whole. But I come out into full consciousness of the outer world and my situation in it, and from time to time I am drained and empty, a hollow vessel, washed up and stranded.

I suppose it all comes back to the one basic thing – I must control and direct my thinking *all the time*, and live always with vision.

— 11th —

What I want to achieve above everything else is complete mastery over myself. Every thought controlled and directed; every emotion channelled into a mainstream of tranquillity and joy. Mastery over myself . . . now I *know* what I have to do. It will occupy every waking minute, calling to order every straying thought; analysing, disciplining, instructing to defeat self-pity, resentment, irritability (oh yes, you *can* be irritable when living alone – you take it out on inanimate objects with much negative muttering).

Now I have a goal I can achieve right here where I am, and presently my horizon will widen as I gain a free mind.

A free mind! What a wonderful clarity to everything that will give. After all, our living is really done within ourselves. It is within that we experience the outward things. So now I am going to be in love again – in love with myself, with the Highest in me. To the beloved I proffer my gifts – an hour without any slip-shod thinking; two hours; half a day; a day . . . a mind under control, an ecstasy of seeking. Then will come the time of dancing, of walking the grey streets in a golden glow, of that extra dimension to everyday things. This is only the beginning . . .

— *12th* —

The wasps seem to spend all their time in and around their nest. What a structure it is! Fixed against the wall of the shed at the edge of the window-frame, it is oval in shape and the material looks like straw, though it is not the colour of straw, but white. I do not know if it is straw, bound with a secretion from their own bodies, because I am afraid to touch it. There are so many of them crawling in and around it. They never come to bother me in the house, and I don't even meet up with them out of doors. Yet there are so many. Some look lazy, lolling about on the window pane in the shed; others are as busy as bees, crawling over and into the nest. I suppose they make their own type of honey. This is the kind of thing you would know, but I cannot ask you.

Do you remember that other wasp summer? There was no sign of a nest then, but crowds of wasps came into the kitchen. We stood saucers of sugar around to divert them. It was amazingly successful. They always gravitated to the saucers and did not bother us at all.

— 13th —

The little black and green caterpillars from the nettles are coming on to the veranda again, seeking a safe place for their transformation. But this year they are behaving differently. Instead of climbing the veranda walls till they reach the ceiling, where they can suspend, they are coming indoors.

The first I knew of it was when I found a half-squashed one on the carpet. Then, when I was sitting here in the rocking chair in the doorway, I saw another attempting to climb the wall of the room. Resolutely I put it outside in the far corner of the window-sill to give it a leg up on its way to the top. Instead it moved swiftly along the sill to the open window, came in, and plopped down on the carpet.

Wish you had been here to see its determination to stay in the room. Moving boldly across the carpet, it tried to climb the skirting board, but the white paint was too slippery a surface, and its attempts were in vain.

It occurred to me that as none of last year's brood survived the winter on the veranda, this year's are seeking safer quarters. But how do they *know*? Can it after all be the same ones, back already in the cycle of life, this time with the stored instinctive knowledge of last year's experience?

Fascinated, I watched the caterpillar return to the carpet and continue its journey of exploration. Well, if it suspended from the ceiling of the room *I* wouldn't mind, and I would be more certain of seeing the butterfly emerge. I

49

tried to place it above the skirting board but as every time I touched it the result was a round ball of caterpillar it was impossible to get it to stay at the base of the wall. Each time a soft plonk on to the carpet where it would remain for some moments before venturing off again.

Finally I had a lovely idea for a safe place and transferred it to the book-case. I left it curled up in a corner, and next time I looked it was full length on the spine of the Jeremy stories. Later I found it suspended in the corner at the back. Great satisfaction for both of us.

— *14th* —

I am very shaken. It is like going back to that January day when the policewoman called. A 'phone call – and V has died. Oh, I am glad that you were not here to bear it. You and she are together now – what a happy, happy reunion.

When I know this, why am I so sad? I am sad for G and for D, of course, but also because V has gone.

Why is death always so momentous, so shattering to the bereaved, as if some dreadfully strange thing has happened, when all the time we know it is the natural end of life on earth? Even when absolutely knowing, as I know, without a shadow of doubt because it is *knowing*, not hope, that another life begins when earth-life ends, the event is traumatic, unbelievable, as if until that moment there was no such happening in the world as death. It has been no stranger to my life, yet always, at first, the terrible, all-engulfing shock . . .

— 15th —

I am trying to cultivate calmness today, but all is unreal again. *Why does death make everything feel so strange when it is a part of life?* I think it must be because emotion is ruling thought when it is thought that should rule emotion. Sorrow is like a sea into which we plunge fully clothed, almost out of our depth, letting the tide sweep us where it will.

Thought says, weep if you will for the one who has gone but know that you are in truth weeping for yourself, and if you cannot weep, bless. Bless the life that has gone from you, embrace it within your heart. And then order your wayward thoughts to obey you, to tell you what truth you know or to cry – 'clinging Heaven by the hems' – for a revelation of truth to assist you on your way, for make your way in your own life you must. With accept-ance, perception, hope, courage and the will to go on, conquering every crisis and gaining self-mastery and other happy achievements. So I counsel myself.

— 20th —

And now Magpie is with you.

I felt sure you would be there to welcome her, you who loved her so much. One by one they will have to come before I do, but I didn't think it would start so soon. It has been so sudden, and I feel so sad to lose her. After she had her teeth out kidney trouble was diagnosed, but she was on tablets and seemed quite well. Then the col-lapse.

I sat up with her all last night. The vet came this morning.

There was nothing he could do, so I had to let her go.

The third grief this year. I see her everywhere with her lovely, funny little ways. Tomorrow I will bury her in one of her favourite places.

⟋ *21st* ⟍

I buried Magpie at dusk in one of her favourite sitting places, under the sycamore tree. It is only her little empty body, but I like to know it is there, in that place. She herself I think of in *another part of the garden*. The invisible part that merges into the realm where the spirit life of animals and all other creatures go.

It is all so very simple and uncomplicated, really; so obvious. Something known deep within the heart. 'Not a sparrow falls without your Father' makes it clear. Every physical body on this earth, be it human or animal, is animated by the Life Spirit, the Father of all. When the Life Spirit returns to its own realm the physical body is dead, but the one who possessed it lives in the spirit body.

I fretted because I could no longer look after her, but even to that the answer came: 'Provision is already made.' Of course. In freedom and happiness she is cared for there as she would be here. They all are. It is part of the law of love, that is never broken there. She will not even have time to miss me because to her now there is no time. Years here could be minutes there.

I think of her in a garden, exploring because it is new. Familiar, too, because it resembles this one, but so much she has not seen or sniffed before, places she has not yet made her own. You go there sometimes, I'm sure. Suddenly she will see you on a path. She will come running up to you in that impetuous way of hers, and then pause, to do the last bit with that funny little sideways walk, talking with her body, sidling along all comical just as she did when she was younger. Do you remember? You must be so glad to see her, to be able to pick her up again . . .

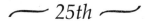 *25th*

I have a new prayer. 'I trust You with my life. I trust You with my life now and for ever. I will not fret. I trust You.'

It is to no distant God that I pray, no unknown being. It is to the Spirit within me. The Spirit that gives me life, that motivates me, sustains and inspires me, and fills all my needs. So close to me; always and for ever with me. Love and comfort flow through me. I relax in it; I rest in the peace of it.

My prayer needs no church, no bowed knee. It is in my heart, all the day long, reaching out to the Spirit within me. I know now that my body is indeed a temple, and that the Spirit of God dwells in it. Sorrow may wash over me like the waves of the sea. I, on my rock, remain, and the tide turns.

Within my temple I am equipped to bear sorrow, survive crisis and all circumstances, and then to cope with each day that follows, with the procession of days to the grand climax.

September

— 12th —

I am sitting in the open doorway, watching the rain. It is the first rain for months. Such light, drifting rain, blowing mistily across the garden on a west wind, not descending solidly to earth to give the plants their much needed refreshment. Nevertheless, it *is* refreshing. After all the heat I could run naked into it, rejoicing. Coming?

From the garden I have had pickings of peas, runner beans, and spinach; I cut broccoli and lift beetroots. The sprouts failed this year, and the carrots, and the one tomato plant I bought from the market simply dropped its flowers. But don't you think I have done quite well?

A dry summer too. I keep all the waste water in buckets in the porch all day and in the evening lug them out to trickle refreshment to the plants that need water most. It is laborious, and in the shed the coiled green snake of hose lies idle. Banned by the Water Authority. I sometimes wonder why we ever bothered to buy it.

And now, after the rain, sunshine. A lit earth and a shadowed sky, white clouds piling against a dark grey horizon and floating by along the sky line, all shapes and sizes, a procession of aerial beauty.

⁓ 16th ⁓

It's myself that bothers me most. Just imagine. Not circumstances, events, life. Me. I need to live free of *myself*. To live with the highest in me, free of confusion, emotion, fret, tension, headache. Free of lumbering, earth-bound thoughts. Free to *live*, to enjoy every moment, every breath, whether savouring a mouthful of food or watching swallows curve pathways in the air. Aware always that the power within will work for me in any and every circumstance. I *know* this. I must cultivate awareness.

⁓ 18th ⁓

I am making progress with self-mastery. I no longer go berserk trying to open tightly sealed plastic packets! They usually open more obligingly now.

When doing something laborious, like the goat beds, I amaze myself by tackling it with calmness and a sense of purpose instead of plunging through it, sweating and muttering, like a demented workaholic. I do one bed at a time, with a break between, instead of two at once, and I feel relaxed, with a sense of achievement.

Next I must bring the load of shopping home on the bike without self-pity, taking my concentration off myself and all the effort involved, slowing down to enjoy the air and the woods and other more companionable thoughts.

What I want now is to live at peace with myself, plus all my material needs.

— *20th* —

Spent a couple of hours on the roof of the goat shed, patching the holes. Got most of the nails in. It's a funny thing that a hammer and a nail are so basically simple that anyone can use them, yet it can be so hard to drive the nail right home.

I remembered the old days while I was doing it. No, not days of wine and roses, but days when I held the ladder praying that the nails you were hammering would go in, days of watching you put the rods down the drain and then running in to pull the plug, praying again that you had succeeded, days of the kettle boiling for endless cups of tea . . . the everyday days with you that are no more.

— *23rd* —

Sitting in the open doorway watching the clouds go by, I found peace again. It was lost for a while, and to regain it is a sweet relief, a restorative balm. From this base I can do what I tell myself in hard moments I must do – proceed calmly.

Everything falls into place. Nothing is adrift, or lost. My life is not in pieces, but like a jigsaw the pieces fit together, to become a complete, comprehensible whole. Maybe I shall even reach the stage when circumstances and events that hitherto have crashed into my calm, temporarily shattering it, will be only an outside storm to my inviolate self within.

— 24th —

I have invented a game for myself. It lifts me above the repetition of routine and gives me a good outlook on life. There is no room for self-pity, no need for it. I am on my mettle. The game is to think of myself as being on an adventure course on earth while you await my return to our heaven home. You – and Magpie. And the others. (I miss that little black cat so much. The memory of her and her sweet, comic ways is with me wherever I look. She was just about everywhere around the place, everywhere I turn.)

The shopping marathon is nothing now I am on an adventure course. I tackle it in the spirit of those who pit their strength and endurance against difficult odds when they undertake certain feats for charity.

Recently I have been thinking about the winter, dreading the difficulties and inconvenience if I get snowed up. Not any more. It will be part of my adventure course. In the old days I never minded – it was always a challenge, even an excitement.

Do you remember the day you walked over ice all the way to the main road to buy liver for the cats? While you were gone I went across the fields, crunching icicles underfoot where grass should have been, and fetched the milk from the village, pulling a week's supply in a crate on a rope behind me like a sledge. Because I couldn't lift it over the field gates I came home by the lane, so deep in a snow drift that I had to walk along the top of the hedge, where the snow was frozen hard.

I enjoyed that excursion, enjoyed the challenge of it. So I will face the coming winter, if it is bad, in the same spirit. And the beauty of it is that my game is not without foundation. The planet earth is not our home; staying here is only a brief and passing interlude in eternity. We all go 'home' in the end, putting off our outer bodies to return with just the 'luggage' of our experiences.

 *25th*

The cock pheasant has returned. Do you remember the winter he roosted in one of the fir trees? Every evening just before dusk he would suddenly appear on top of the bank from the further field, then slowly advance across the garden, caution in every inch of him, until he reached his special tree. A pause, then a tremendous flutter, and either by sheer luck or immense good judgement his heavy body would land on the lowest branch. Then all caution was thrown to the winds as he disappeared under a dark spray of leaves, for he would shout his safe arrival to the world.

I could never understand why he was not careful to keep his roosting place a secret – but no, for several minutes that crackle of a call, so tingling to the blood, resounded in the quiet evening. Perhaps it was triumph, for achieving that branch was no mean feat.

He has called from the fields from time to time during the summer, but now he comes to the garden again, pecking under the bird-table and even making his way to the bird-boards you made on the banks.

How handsome he looked this autumn morning, with the sun mellow and the air soft. Catching a glimpse of his back in the long grass he looked like a big brown hen until the sun glinted and burnished those feathers to the richest of golden brown like newly coloured autumn leaves. Then his emerald neck and ruby head emerged, and all the elegance of him, and as always I watched, entranced.

In the background were the two white goats, still as

statues, Lucy sitting in the dusty place she had made under the fir trees, one foreleg stretched restfully in front of her, long beard trailing it, a smug look of contentment on her face, and Snowdrop standing behind, just as smug.

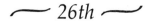 *26th*

There were six buzzards floating against the clear blue back-drop of sky this morning, four of them smaller than the others. I wanted to run and tell you that the pair from the woods must have brought their young. Perhaps it was their first long flight.

I watched them dip and soar and float on those marvellous out-stretched wings, the little ones as adept as their parents. The parents were flying fairly low, at the usual height we see them, but the young ones went much higher – so high that at times they became the merest specks. They all stayed for awhile, and then slowly drifted back towards the woods.

29th

Sometimes it is necessary to sit in a very small space. The corner of the sofa, its back slanted across the centre of the room (I have changed the furniture round) is comfortable and feels safe. Above me is the window through which, sitting down, I can see only a bit of sky and the tip of a tall conifer. I am in an enclosed world. It gives a feeling of security, of peace. There is no need to move for a time.

October

~ 14th ~

I cycled down to the woods today to gather leafy twigs for the goats. There are still leaves on many of the trees, some still green, although the recent gales have stripped vast numbers and scattered them everywhere in brown and golden heaps, making frilly borders of them along each side of the lane. There must be thousands. I was lucky and gathered easily for the goats from a large oak branch tossed down by the wind and loaded with leaves beautifully mottled in green and yellow. How those two grabbed at them when I got back!

Do you remember how they used to sense your approach up the lane, staring alert-eyed towards the bank that hid you from view, and then rush to the gate to pull at the branches in your laden rucksack? And the pond – do you remember the pond? I climbed on to the bank today to look. They have been thinning the trees behind it and clearing the water of weed, and the clear shining depths reflect the slim grey trunks of the leafless poplars. I have no words to describe the fiery beech tree on the left bank. It was truly alight with colour.

The poplars made me a little sad, remembering them as

your favourite tree, and then I remembered the time we went across the marshy ground to the stream and sank into the boggy mud, only extricating ourselves by struggling out of our wellington boots. It is like remembering a dream. One day I shall awake and know this present time as a dream also.

— 21st —

It has been very hard for G and D since V went. To think that this time last year they were here for their autumn holiday, and there were five of us. Within a year you two gone, and Magpie too. My comfort is in thinking of the lovely reunion of you and V. How very, very happy she must have been to see you. She tried to find comfort in belief, but hers was hope compared to my conviction – my *knowing*. (Only by personal experience can you *know*.)

When she grieved for you and took her little posies to your body's resting place in that peaceful churchyard above the sea, I remember saying to her that she would see you again – that one day she was going to have a lovely surprise. 'Well, I hope so, Freda,' she said. Now she *knows* . . . but oh, how soon!

— 23rd —

D and G cancelled the holiday they were all to spend down here, but came to see me for a few days. It was courageous of them, and required a lot of effort – that long drive on the familiar route without V. I was so glad to see them and appreciated the effort they had made. When they had settled in, it proved to be a very pleasant visit. We talked and talked. We sat up till midnight, talking much of you and V. I took them on walks, which they enjoyed, G discovering fox-holes and D picking late flowers, and although it is October the weather did them proud. One day was like summer. It only broke the day they went back.

— *26th* —

Today it rained all the morning, but by midday cleared quite suddenly. All the depressing greyness gone, and the sun shining. I am sitting in the open doorway of the veranda. The sky is a deep, deep blue, and part of it is paved in little white fragments of clouds, like cobblestones. The hawthorn tree down the field sparkles all over with diamond raindrops, and every blade of the shining grass holds a gem. October – and the sun is hot.

— *31st* —

I have lived 277 days without you. Looking back over them, my mind automatically blacks out the time before that. I still cannot consciously allow myself to live again in thought the days when you were here, unless I am sharing a memory with you here in this book. To look into the days ahead is to look into a desert without an oasis.

I am only safe within the day. 'I can get through till nightfall,' wrote Robert Louis Stevenson, and how true that is. It is all that is necessary really, except that, as the days continue, there is a need, sometimes an urge, to make each one worthwhile. In the end it becomes essential to achieve more than performing the routine tasks, more than just survival. Some satisfaction has to be injected into that basic necessity. It can be the fragile outline of a plan, an effort made for somebody else, a new interest discovered, a sudden conscious awareness of beauty.

One sleeps better at the end of a day that has had some satisfaction in it.

November

9th

The dark evenings are here. I am thankful that looking after the goats entails evening jobs too. The house seems strange rather than cosy now with the curtains drawn, the bright fluorescent light in the empty kitchen and the middle room quiet in its soft, rosy light. No sound until the 'fridge starts up, oddly comforting as it puts heart into the kitchen, or Hudson asks for more to eat. No movements unless I make them.

I miss the constant hiss of the kettle boiling, the tinkle of your teaspoon against the cup. I cannot drink tea as often as you did. The bedroom is a dark cavern – you are not even in there with your book.

There is a kind of expectancy now when I sit down, as if it is still this time last year and at any moment the door will open and you will drift through to the bathroom or to make more tea. I no longer 'see' you as I did in the early days, but have this strange feeling that the door will suddenly open. If I am not careful it becomes frightening, as if I half expect some unknown person to come in. I can only sit in that room of an evening if I am fully occupied

– completely absorbed in a book, writing, or really interested in a special television programme.

I go to bed earlier. Remember my late nights? Sometimes you were getting up for yet another cup of tea when I came in to bed. Then in the middle of the night I would half wake to the smell of frying onions as you prepared a late, late supper or a very early breakfast. I miss the thump when you returned to bed – I miss having to grab at the bedclothes before they slid off me. Sometimes I think I hear you breathing, and then I realise that it is Kate, fast asleep in a hollow of blankets.

I go to bed with the radio now, turned low, and fall asleep to distant music or the murmur of a voice. I find this comforting and relaxing. And for a while Kate – little Kate, the comforter – is curled in the crook of my arm.

⌐ *15th* ⌐

It is a beautiful morning. I saw it begin. A thin mist slid silently away across the fields, hazy with early, tepid sunshine. Now the sun has come out big and strong and bright, and burning with warmth in the odd corner where the fresher November air cannot temper it.

I am sitting in the open doorway of the veranda, basking in it as if summer had returned. The green, green grass still shimmers in the lightly breathing air with sparkling droplets of mist, flashing brilliantly in the sun.

I am at peace. This is not something I would share with you. There is room in the doorway for only one chair, and if you were here you would not want to sit in it. You preferred to sit indoors rather than out, even in summer.

I think perhaps the outdoors was too big for you. The vast horizon can be overwhelming. When I was young and in a town there was no horizon in the streets, but I remember how, on a bright day, I would get the impression of vastness, of everything so much bigger, larger than life, and no hidden places. I didn't like the feeling.

Here, where the skyline encircles us, I feel safe, as if enclosed.

Did you notice? I said 'us' instead of 'me'. I still do that in conversation with others, to people I meet at the bus stop. 'We,' I say, when referring to things at home. Quite unconsciously.

⌐ *16th* ⌐

Another landmark looms ahead. Christmas. I am collecting cards and presents for those to whom we send cards and presents.

How you hated this season of the year. The commercial build-up, the work-load of housewives, the anti-climaxes . . . there was no end to it. I even gave up making Christmas puddings. The only things you liked about it were the old films on television. I shall not watch them this year. They will be the one aspect of Christmas to remind me of you. For the rest, we carried on with our usual routine, and of course with the animals that is easy. Just a treat for the cats, extra biscuits for the goats, sweets for you, sweets for me. So it will be this year, except no sweets for you.

Viewing it from the distance of weeks, I cannot see any heartache in it. I shall not mind being alone. I am alone every day. I cannot understand the fuss that is made about 'being alone at Christmas'. Everyone can make their own little Christmas if they wish, and there must be many like me who can accommodate themselves to being alone.

There is no sense in being a martyr to Christmas. I shall not be one.

— 18th —

I love to watch the slow, stately procession of huge white and dark clouds, with the sun behind them, across the pale blue November sky. The very slowness of movement almost hypnotises me. The sight has a soothing quality. I have a wide view from the wall of window in the middle room. Sometimes at a first glance the clouds do not seem to be moving at all, and then I become aware that they *are*, imperceptibly, but steadily and continuously.

Like the clouds, the days merge into each other, almost losing their individual identity. Unlike the clouds they race by, and yet I feel I am only marking time.

— 22nd —

The seed catalogues have arrived, punctuating the month with memory. Such memories do not hurt quite so much now. I feel I should think of you more, instead of escaping from memory.

You were very close yesterday, weren't you? I *knew* you were here. You were *pleased!* The bike man said Revel needed a new tyre, and is to do it soon, and *then* I remembered that you had foreseen this and already bought the tyre. I tried to remember where you put it, then very quickly found it in the cupboard, and *then*, suddenly, you were quite close, pleased I had found it.

Once again your forethought has paid off. You always prepared for emergencies – I did not always agree with your advance shopping and laying in of things, but you were right. I am glad I shan't have to buy a tyre because there has been a lot of expense lately.

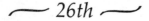

26th

Nearly December, and the weather is frosty. Cold, brilliant days and sharp starlit nights. With the sun so low in the sky the brightness of the light is almost startling. In the brightness this Sunday morning I cycled to the woods to gather oak leaves for the goats from the fallen branches. They are all brown and crisp now, but the goats crunch them like biscuits.

The ride down was not pleasant. The easterly air-stream lapped my ears as icy as water, and the sun's rays through the right-hand hedge flickered before my eyes like the flashes of light in migraine. The wood was still, the tall bare trees dignified, the cattle on the hillside carved against the skyline, and in the low field by the stream the bright-backed sheep were rimmed in light.

I lost my gloves, found them, and came home filling my eyes with the beauty of the day, the sun hot on my back. Only the grass is green now, vividly green, and the dark green firs, the lichen-patched trunks of the older ash trees, and a few oaks whose trunks are tightly wrapped in ivy. The beeches are black, with finger-tip buds of brown on their boughs, and the stiff brown stems of the beheaded bracken stand up stiffly in the shorn hedge. I saw catkins already half an inch long on the hazels.

Today I wore my pink woolly hat with the elastic round the edge, but as I went along the elastic lost its grip and the hat worked loose. When I noticed my shadow walking companionably beside me as I pushed the bike uphill, it had gone into a peak and looked like a clown's hat.

— 27th —

Hard frosts at night. White fields and ice-patched roads in the mornings. I cannot remember such weather here so early. Opinions about the coming winter are divided, and completely opposite. There are those who think that the early onset of cold weather means it will go on like this, only worse. A hard winter. Others quote an old country saying, 'If there's ice in November, enough for a duck, there'll be a winter of rain and muck.' Most people opt for the cold weather 'to kill the germs'. Me, I prefer a more comfortable temperature.

— 28th —

So heavy the frost last night the fields look as if they have a covering of snow. The black bullocks with their sad white faces mooch along by the hedge, seeking tufts of grass still green.

Each day the sun has appeared early, melting the frost and bringing a measure of comfort, but today a huge bank of cloud has shut it out. Now the sky is smooth and colourless all over. Gone the beauty of yesterday when I went out, the sun coming up over the hill with sudden radiance as I passed the brown tangle of woods, its slanting rays making a mysterious golden haze under the trees ahead, only to vanish like breath as I reached there.

— 29th —

A sad-glad day. I took the new tyre you bought all that time ago to the bike man, to be fitted on Revel. All wrapped up in soft paper and carefully stored away till needed. It was strange, handling it now – the one final thing you have done for me. Sad-glad . . . a feeling of unshed tears with warmth behind them.

December

— 12th —

I missed you yesterday. Everything was difficult, or went wrong. A day of one thing after another. In the morning I had to get the vet to Lucy, who has a cold. The second visit. She improved, and then seemed to have a set-back, but this time her temperature was down. She is very sorry for herself and not eating much.

It was a day of storm-force wind, so Snowdrop had to stay in too. But did she! While I was taking a bucket of water into the shed she dodged out. The wind was terrific. I slammed the door shut and dashed after her. Round and round the place we went, the wind tearing at us all the time, but she would not be caught. I needed you so badly to head her off, but eventually I cornered her and bundled her in.

Then as I went to close the door the top hinge came off and the door leaned drunkenly against me. I managed with some difficulty in the teeth of the wind to screw it back on again.

I cut bramble for the goats and mislaid one of my gardening gloves, so spent more time in the wind searching. At least I found it. Then I noticed that the nuts I put out for the blue tits were low. (I bought a bird feeder in the market last week and have hung it against one of the conifers.) Came in for the nuts and then dropped the lot in long grass! It took some time to winkle them all out and back into the bag.

All day and all night the wind raged. I prayed the goat shed would stand up to it. It did. I was so glad not to lose the electricity. Power lines are down all over the place, but our supply remained. This morning the wind is dropping.

— 25th —

For me there has been no Christmas. Not even one to forget. Lucy has been so very ill. The vet has been coming, and I have been hand-feeding her, and going to her in the night. She lies in the straw, all floppy. Then she takes the food and holds her head up. Hope rises . . .

— 26th —

Lucy's breathing is the only sound in the goat shed. Snowdrop sits in her pen, quiet and good. The windows are covered with grain bags to keep out the cold. The lamp hangs from the high nail. The breathing, the rasping breathing, is terrible to hear . . . She snuggles against me, lets me cradle her head.

— 27th —

Lucy died this morning. She was dying when the vet called to give her another injection. So this time it had to be a lethal one. So quietly she passed, without knowing, her head against me. I felt weak and shaken. I propped her head up so that for Snowdrop she still appeared alive, that lovely 'smiling' look on her face that she always had when she was happy.

I felt empty, lost, then pushed myself into a frenzy of activity and went at once up to the fir trees, that favourite place, to dig a grave for her. It seemed it had to be done at once, at once, because there was only me to bury her and I had to do it, had to prove to myself that I could manage it. I felt that if I did not do it straightaway I could not do it at all.

The digging was easy enough in the soft earth there, and it was done within an hour. Hudson sat beside me while I dug. I came in to rest and Kate climbed into my lap and licked me.

The worst part was to come.

I shut Snowdrop in the other half of the goat shed and tried to manoeuvre Lucy on to the wheelbarrow. I couldn't do it, Eric. I couldn't do it. Nor was I in any state to go for outside help. I dragged her out of the shed by her forelegs, her head flopping, and then over the grass where I sat her against the wall till dusk. Then, little by little, I dragged her to the resting place.

I lined it with thick brown grain bags and straw, and covered her with straw, and wrapped her head in sweet-smelling hay. Before I could finish putting all the earth back it grew dark. I stood the lamp on the path and finished the job.

Now I feel too weak to move, but I must go to Snowdrop . . .

— 28th —

You came to me last night . . . Your voice actually came through to me. For a moment the wavelengths must have merged . . .

I am stronger now.

— 30th —

The weather has been grey and cold. Snowdrop is fretting. Because she cannot find Lucy in the shed she is convinced she must be out of doors, and she stands at the window staring, calling. She was very agitated at midday and only snatched at her food. I could not comfort her. It's not me she wants. It's Lucy.

I tell myself that this time will pass like all the other times. Happy times, sad times, good and bad times – they all pass. That is my rope. The movement of time is merciful, not disastrous, as you so often felt. But I hate to see Snowdrop like this, and ask myself if I should have allowed her to see me drag Lucy's body from the shed. But how could I have inflicted that horrifying picture on her nervous disposition? She must in time become adjusted, even as the sheep adjust when their lambs are taken away. I have watched them grieve, always looking, constantly calling. It passes in a day, two days. Will it be the same for Snowdrop? She lived with Lucy seven years.

— 31st —

What a strange year it has been. Four deaths. Yours, V, Magpie and Lucy. You at the beginning of the year, Lucy at the end.

Over all the years there has been so much sorrow, but looking back one great thing remains – my experiences during that terrible time in the 'fifties did prove to me for the first time beyond doubt that the dead live. Even the animals.

At every death something in me dies a little, and at the same time I am aware that something else has been strengthened. But how glad I shall be when all the dying is done . . . mine too . . .

January

1st

'What, you still here?' I say to myself.
Still surviving . . . as my old boss used to say.

2nd

This New Year I am having to think very seriously about life. Not only about my survival, but how to make this last phase worthwhile. I cannot just exist. Life is for *living*. It is *a personal experience not dependent on anyone else*. We each live *our own* life. I must *live fully, I myself*, within my capabilities.

First, I have to form a new relationship with Snowdrop, a companionable relationship now she has lost her companion. I have already begun. I am giving her a lot of attention, having little games in the shed with her now she cannot butt heads with Lucy. She has to stay in because of the weather.

When I go over there she 'talks' a lot. This is something entirely new. She had her 'talking' times before, but it was not every time I went into the shed. She looks in Lucy's empty pen, and I immediately divert her. I bring her oak leaves and bramble in addition to her meals, and she enjoys these as usual. When she stands she looks so alone in the empty shed. It is hard, but we shall get over it. Both of us.

This coming year, this new decade, I must cultivate three things. Firstly a constant awareness of Power – the Power in my highest self within me; secondly creative planning; thirdly a great *expectation*. I must use the Power in every circumstance by positive thought, I must make plans for my life, and I must expect pleasant, fulfilling happenings. Expectation is stimulating, thrilling and – magnetic. I must never shut the door on life; never close my mind to it.

These are not New Year resolutions. Each day is new. It is just the way I will face up to all the days still ahead. Although you will not be here, we shall eventually share all that happens. We shall have so much to tell each other! I shall walk more firmly through this year, and achieve things, and when the shadow of your absence steals across a moment of enjoyment it will only be like passing through sunshine and shade on a summer day.

— 3rd —

A week since Lucy died, and we are finding peace, Snowdrop and I. The peace of acceptance. Her time of fretting is done; she goes quietly along with her routine. Her enthusiasm for life has waned, her exuberant boisterousness, but she lives and accepts, and presently some of her enthusiasm will return. A biscuit treat no longer matters now – she who could not eat biscuits fast enough when they were offered. But she eats most of her food. She does not particularly mind whether she is indoors or out, and when out will go in of her own accord sometimes – a thing she never did.

We go down the field together in the late afternoon and I, at least, pretend Lucy is just out of sight – behind the caravan, up on the bank. She had such a knack of disappearing from view – I was always checking up on her. I wait while Snowdrop eats. She delves into the thick, matted grass round the edge of the field much as usual, concentrating on it, and pulls at bramble in the wild part.

I thought she had forgotten her loss, but suddenly today there came a distant sound on the silent winter air, probably one of the sheep. It was not all that distinct, and Snowdrop stopped eating and stiffened, looking up, all eyes and ears. Then she ran fast, back up the field into the garden. When I got there she was standing motionless. Words could not have told me more plainly that she had expected to find Lucy. It nearly broke my heart. Still, things are better.

8th

Brilliant day, stolen from spring. I let Snowdrop out early and was actually able to take the garden-chair down to where she sunned herself by the goat shed to keep her company while I drank a cup of coffee. A day to lift the spirits, and yet sorrow intruded. I wondered how I would have been feeling now if Lucy had not died too . . . I ask myself for whom I grieve. It will soon be your anniversary.

9th

M's anniversary today. Every detail of that day is so clear, although it is thirteen years ago. Sadness is inevitable as

I remember. Up to that time there were fifteen of us here – three people, twelve animals. Now there is one person and three animals.

The greatest blessings we have are, in my opinion, Life Itself, the concealment of the future, and sleep. The power to breathe and think and move – how can we not rejoice in it? And just suppose that this time last year I had known exactly what that year would bring . . . how could I have got through? As for sleep, it is bliss.

⸺ *12th* ⸺

A wet shopping day. Rain flowed and sheeted off pavements like the incoming tide on a beach. I squelched in and out of shops.

'Now all you need is a pack-horse outside,' said the girl in the supermarket as I piled cat-food tins into my already loaded bags.

I smiled. 'I've got a bike,' I said.

Lugging the lot, I staggered out with the load to my trusty steed.

On the homeward journey the rain eased, and I rode through curtains of drizzle. A dead squirrel lay by my front wheel on the main road. Intact, but for a damaged head, its fur and bushy tail still beautiful. I moved it to the verge. Bless you, little one . . . how did you come to be crossing there, so far from the woods?

When I reached home I found the bag of flour was wet, and had burst. Flour over everything. (You would have been prepared, equipped with thick paper to wrap it in. Me, I didn't think.)

Now the rain has gone. The night is still. When I went to give Snowdrop her supper the sky looked like a spring sky, all blue and white, a sprinkling of stars among the gentle white clouds.

Snowdrop has settled down now without Lucy. When I took her out in the lane today – a special treat – she was exuberant on our return and leapt at me, pretending to butt.

— 13th —

Sunshine. I bask in it in the veranda doorway, and find peace.

The blue hyacinth you gave me for indoors is blooming again. I have it on the window-sill in the middle room. Life goes on . . .

— 17th —

When peeling the potatoes there was a medium-sized one with a small one attached to the top – just like a body and a head. I couldn't resist making it into a 'little man', peeling the body part and sticking in split peas to look like buttons, and hollowing out eyes, nose and mouth in the 'head', on which I stuck a carrot-end to make a cap. Then matchsticks for arms and legs. Such a jolly little man – in fact I called him Mr Jolly. I sat him on the kitchen window-sill on top of the flask, and every time I glance at him he makes me smile. A good omen. If a potato can make me smile I can be much more light-hearted this year. Must cultivate it.

— 20th —

A letter from D to read with my morning cup of tea. How cheering it is to receive a nice chatty letter, especially on a dull day like this.

I opened Snowdrop's door early as it is so mild, but immediately afterwards a thin mist drifted across the fields. I cannot see beyond the further hedge. Snowdrop will only come out if the mist clears, but she can stand at the door and look out at the world for a change.

Lots of blue tits are tumbling over one another to gain a place on the bird-feeder for nuts. I was thrilled to see a greenfinch among them. It is the first greenfinch I have seen in the garden.

— 23rd —

This time last year these were the last few days of your life on earth. They are very vivid to me, like a photographic memory, yet at the time I did not consciously absorb the incidents of that week. Now I feel I am living them again. There is a sweetness now in the muted sadness. I feel very close to you. Once again you are sitting in your chair in the middle room drinking tea or rolling a cigarette, or watching the television news. Once again I 'see' you walking in and out of the rooms; emerging from the door of the caravan; coming down the hill with your red rucksack.

Two things happened that week that gave you immense pleasure. I remember them so well, and they give me a warm feeling now because they made you happy. One was a late-night film; the other was the white owl.

I came across the film in the part of the programme I seldom glanced at because it was after midnight. It was your sort of film, and I knew you would like it, and would probably be up in the night, anyway, so I told you about it. You watched it with great pleasure. Even now I can remember the enthusiasm with which you recounted it to me.

And the owl! That was really strange. We often saw it when we first came here, flying low along the hedge at dusk, but had not seen it for years. Then that evening you came in all excited and told me, 'I've just seen the white owl! I wanted to call you, but it went.' You described its flight to me, where you saw it; your face lit up. We talked about it, and hoped it would come again. I said I would watch for it each evening.

It came that one time. I never have seen it since.

⟋ *27th* ⟍

Your anniversary . . . a whole year has passed. Or is it half a life-time since you were here? There are still all the days ahead, but I do not see them now. I have expanded my consciousness . . . I try to live in that expansion. Where I saw a burden of days I now see a bright vista of eternity, a beautiful timelessness where past, present and future are all one, where nothing is lost and everything is safe for ever. Mentally I am travelling in it, and travelling light, unencumbered with the luggage of fret and fear, of self-pity and rebellion, of guilt and tension and all the paraphernalia of worry and distress.

Oh yes, I may be sad at times, bone weary with shopping, bogged in trivia in this immediate world, but in my mind and heart and self I can *soar* into that new awareness.

I remember how you used to pass through the kitchen, saying cheerfully, 'All right, then?' To which today I cheerfully reply, 'I'm fine.'

I do not look at the days any more. I do not know how many or how few there are, but . . . see you.